Jo's Journey

Scarlet Jo Hanson

Contents

Introduction

Hello, and thank you for picking up this book.

First and foremost, these stories are about men because I date men. It is NOT intended to be a man-bashing book, nor is it gender specific. I have been mistreated by women (a business partner, life-long friends, besties who betrayed me with MY boyfriend, etc.). These short stories can apply to any relationship situation. The stories described by my experience are not discriminatory racially, religiously, by height, weight, or any other discriminating factor. They are simply interesting encounters that I find humorous and enlightening in hindsight.

Finding humor in life's events has always proved helpful for me. Life lessons should not be taken lightly, and the emotional upheaval needs to be addressed. Making jokes and being able to laugh about the situation has typically worked in my favor. When I lose my sense of humor, I will probably be brain-dead. We don't want that - Yikes.

Divorce after many years is difficult at best. Hurt and anger are foremost in one's mind and attitude at that time. Many years post-divorce, I know that burden has been heavy and has slowed my recovery.

You will notice, as you read these encounters, that I tried

to be something everyone else wanted or needed. I now need to continue to discover the charming, delightful, creative, energetic, risk-taking person that I truly am.

Even though many have knocked me down and pushed me around, I always come back ready to swing again. So here I am --trying a new avenue to get back on the track that works for me. Write the book I started years ago, get the garment I developed back in the marketplace, do more yoga, play more golf, travel more often, and do whatever it takes to be me. The failures and bumps I had in the past will no longer define me. I will move forward and keep on!

My hope is that you will find situations, ideas, thoughts, and feelings that resonate with you. If one person is touched, learns from my mistakes, or realizes they are not alone, I'm thrilled.

I now believe I am worthy of a wonderful relationship, but I must persist until I find the one who can hold on to the emotional, deep-feeling, sensitive, and fun person that I am.

I want to be ME. You can be YOU!

Lovingly, Scarlet

Jo's Journey

1

Never Believe the Sob Story

Steven

Like many of you out there, I pride myself on being a pretty good judge of character. When you meet someone on the internet and get to know each other a bit over email, you sacrifice the benefits that come along with meeting in person. Picking up on body language and having direct social interaction helps us judge how much we feel we can trust a person. And yet, I also think that in some ways, you get to know someone better when you both have some time to craft your thoughts into the written word and get past the petty small talk that can dominate an initial face-to-face meeting.

Steven was a businessman from Chicago with whom I'd been emailing back and forth for a few weeks after we found each other on a popular dating website. Photos on an internet dating profile should be taken with at least a little grain of salt. If Steven's pictures were even remotely representative of reality, he was literally tall, dark, and quite handsome. I'd say above average looking. That's always a plus.

He had an eight-year-old son, and we bonded over our mutual experience of parenting. He worked at a company that did contract work globally. He seemed quite intelligent, and wonder of wonders, actually used correct grammar. I know that's a somewhat shallow point to judge a potential mate on, but I can't help it; my interest in a man practically disappears into thin air when I open a message to see, "YOUR really pretty" or "Meeting in person is better THEN emailing." Call me a dork, but correct grammar usage earns a man big points in my book. (*My book - ha ha*)

Steven informed me that he was going out of the country for business, but he wanted to meet for a date after he got back in a week or so. I agreed. I couldn't help but be cautiously optimistic about this one. I got a good vibe from him, and it seemed like we had a lot in common.

A couple of days later, I received an email from Steven that I figured would be a pleasant update on his trip or a quick note to let me know that he was looking forward to our date. I was wrong. Instead, this is the correspondence I received:

"Scarlet,

You'll never believe this (These words were a red flag) but my son and I just arrived in Africa and they took all of our stuff...our bags, our passports, and all of our money. Could you please send me $5,000?

-Steven"

I was in shock, and needless to say, my heart sank. A bad date can be demoralizing enough, but this took it to a new level.

This was worse than any rejection, adding insult to injury with a sense of betrayal. I felt like a sucker, because that's exactly what he apparently thought I was. No wonder he was such a good writer! He convinces people to give him money over email for a living.

During our brief interaction, I thought Steven was sharing an intimate part of himself with me. I had shared a part of myself and allowed myself to get my hopes up. As a single woman, it is easy to romanticize the future, despite the risk of disappointment.

My feelings of disappointment were fleeting, however. I brushed it off easily enough and chalked it up to experience. At least this was something new and, on some level, even somewhat amusing. Steven's ruse wasn't the most clever. I wondered if this approach had actually worked for him in the past; were there women out there who actually fell for this? I decided it would be best to just ignore it, figuring he'd get the hint. I had no intention of sending large sums of money to a complete stranger, and that would be the end of it.

Wrong again.

A couple of days later, I received another email from him, this time simply saying:

"I can't believe you'd leave me like this in my time of need. You couldn't even bother to respond?"

I was amazed. He was actually getting on my case about

email etiquette, like I was supposed to RSVP to the Take Me for All I'm Worth party at which I would be the guest of honor? The nerve of this guy! How stupid did he think I was? Well, I thought, if it's a response he wants, then that's what he'll get. This is what I wrote:

"Dear Steven,

I'm SO sorry I didn't write back sooner. The craziest thing happened. On my way to Western Union to wire you the money. I was in a terrible car accident and I'm in the hospital! My insurance won't cover all of the hospital bills. Could you PLEASE send **ME** *$7,000?*

Thanks"

An hour later, there was a message in my inbox that read:

"Fuck you."

I can't begin to imagine who this guy was or what his life was like, but every time I think about our little exchange, I can't help but smile to myself with a touch of smug satisfaction. At least I was able to give him a little taste of his own medicine. Call me old-fashioned, but I think you should at least take a girl out for a dinner or two before popping the *"Can you send me 5,000 dollars?"* question.

~~~~

Coping idea -- Speaking of Old Fashioned, how about
~~~~

one right now?

A wonderful whiskey with bitters! Perfect!

2

People Allowed in Your Life are Contagious; Choose Wisely and Cut Quickly

Wayne

Few things make my heart happier than a group ride through the countryside that takes on a breezy beauty when seen from a motorcycle. Yep, I'm a small lady (*and I do mean lady*) who would take a Harley over a Schwinn any day.

Imagine my delight when a friend invited me to help his retail team run their pop-up stores during the annual Sturgis Motorcycle Rally in South Dakota. For a little over a week, Sturgis turns into a biker's dream come true. Bikers from all over the globe and from all socioeconomic backgrounds hang out to celebrate all things motorcycle. Rides through the hills, music of all genres, biker attire (or lack of same), and bikes that are out of this world. Even a couple of Hell's Angels came into the store while I was working. (*I stayed clear of them - not my cup of tea*). Happily, I did meet some interesting men who were interested in me. I can talk and ride "bikes" after all!!

One such man was from Wisconsin. He came in more

than once and sought me out. He eventually persuaded me to give him my phone number. Since we were both bikers, I thought it was fine. There is a bit of built-in trust if you're a fellow biker.

Once back home, he did contact me. He told me about a ride with some friends in Wisconsin and asked me to join them. It would involve a few days on the bike. Fine with me. I had a "big boy bike" (*1450 cc Softail Deluxe, lava red, white wall tires - yeah baby*). A group ride is very comfortable for me, even with people I don't know well. There is a certain camaraderie that riders have immediately. There are unwritten rules that most riders typically observe. No concern there.

The concern: how would I get to Wisconsin? It's a long ride from Michigan to Milwaukee. Riding through or around Chicago is not exactly a delight on a motorcycle. That would be a congested five-hour ride. Another option was the high-speed ferry, which goes from Muskegon to Milwaukee. We decided Wayne would bring his bike trailer and meet me at the boat dock in Milwaukee. His drive would take about an hour and a half. I would travel an hour to Muskegon, then catch the two-and-a-half-hour ride on the ferry across Lake Michigan.

The day of my departure, the rain comes, and it pours and pours.

YIKES!!! But I'm a biker who knows a commitment is a commitment. Get on the bike, girl! Thankful I have riding rain gear, new tie downs to hold the bike on the ferry, a strong luggage case packed with all my weekend trappings, a printed map of the area, and my ferry ticket. I was in pretty good shape for the trek.

A new concern meets me head on. In the pouring rain, bike travel is slow, and the roads are more dangerous. My paper map (in my pocket) couldn't help me and Mariah (*yes, my bike's name is Mariah - like the wind, not the singer*) had no GPS on her. I knew my careful planning was getting thrown right out the window (no pun intended), and it didn't take long before I found myself frightened and worried about getting to the launch site all on my own.

Somewhere along the way, I made a wrong turn and ended up in a neighborhood with only dead-end and curvy streets everywhere. I'm in Muskegon, but I see beautiful homes, lots of trees, suburbia extraordinaire. Obviously, not the docks for a ferry across Lake Michigan.

Stop the bike, pull out the printed map (which immediately smears in the rain), memorize where I need to go, put the map back, try again. Shit. Shit. Shit. Still not right. I'm frustrated, cold, and wet. Stop again, try again. Nope. Closer and closer. Try again.

Whew!!!

The docks!

YAY!

As I passed the gate, guess what I saw? The ferry pulling away from the dock. NOOOOOOO. After all that! What the ….

I pulled into the lot, parked the bike, and ran in to see what I could do.

There was another ferry in five hours. The ferry route is from Muskegon to Milwaukee, turn around, come back, and then do it again. I could catch the next one! No extra charge. Great! Okay - time to call Wayne and tell him what happened.

I say, "Hello, bad news. Because of rain, directions, etc., I missed the ferry but can catch the next one." Then I explained the ferry system and once it returned, I could board and be on my way.

His response, "How ridiculous, you can't get there on time! What am I going to do for five hours in Milwaukee??? Just forget it."

Me, "What?"

Click. End of conversation.

Well, I guess you can't make mistakes with Wayne. That was a very rude, short, temperamental response in my book (*now he's in my book, ha*). Good to know. What's that adage about untangling the Christmas tree lights -- You need to slowly work the knots out. You don't throw a fit; you need to be gentle and patient. Perhaps Wayne has never untangled tree lights.

As I headed back home, in the still pouring rain, my

temper kicked in. He was very unkind, and his response was one-sided and short-sighted. I didn't miss the boat on purpose. There was certainly a way to still make it happen since the ride with his friends wasn't until the next day. But he apparently showed his true colors when a minor snag arose in the plan.

What did I do? On my way home, I did the math. He had a 90-minute drive to the docks; my ferry ride was two and a half hours. HE HADN'T EVEN LEFT HOME YET! OMG - more pissed! Once I arrived home, still wet and angry, I wrote him an apology email explaining how ditzy I was. Ha Ha. _WRONG._ I didn't want to speak with him, so I sent an email telling him exactly what I thought of his response and told him __not__ to contact me again. Seemed clear enough, right?

A few weeks later, I received an email from him inviting me to Wisconsin. My response, "Wait, should I reiterate how you treated me? You were the one who couldn't do math. You hadn't even left home. Now you want me to try that, again? NOT A CHANCE IN HELL."

Is this how all Wisconsin men react? Or Biker guys? Well, read on. There's more of both!

~~~~~

Coping Tool -- Call your biker friends and ride! If it's raining, sit home reading a funny book (pun intended), and enjoy a glass of fine wine!
~~~~~

Scarlet Jo Hanson

3

If Someone Likes You, You'll Know. If They Don't, You'll Be Confused

Eric

An Engineer. Yes, a real train engineer -- Choo Choo.

Bike Week in Sturgis, SD is where I met Eric. It was such a great opportunity to meet men with so much in common (or so I thought). Since I am a bit adventurous, I was attracted to biker guys.

Eric came into the store a few times, and we were able to get together twice outside the store. On one outing, we went for a ride on his bike. It was a beautiful bike and a beautiful ride. Another time we putzed around Sturgis doing some shopping and enjoying a libation. IIe was very attractive. He sported a ponytail, which I thought was sexy. As my luck would have it, he lived in Arizona. A state very distant from Michigan. But when we left Sturgis, we agreed to stay in touch and see where our connection might lead.

Once back home, we spent hours talking on the phone,

expressing our thoughts and wishes about life in general. Eventually, we agreed it was time to see each other again. We made plans for him to come to my house for a visit. At the time, I had a four bedroom home on a small inland lake just north of Grand Rapids. It was a great house for entertaining.

I was at the airport to pick him up the moment he arrived. We then headed to my house to get him settled in. When I showed him his room, there was a definite pause in his presence. He said with a big sigh, "OK."

In my mind, I went, "Hmmmmm." Was he thinking he was going to jump into bed with me? Was he thinking we would be sleeping together? Was he disappointed? He didn't say anything else, and I didn't ask.

In hindsight, why didn't I say, "Did you think I was that easy? You think there's sex before you buy me dinner?" (*I'm a bit smarter now than I was then - I hope.*)

Since it was summer, I suggested we go outside and sit by the lake. At the time, I had a home-based business, so I had to answer and make a few phone calls while Eric was visiting. I mentioned this to him ahead of time, and he assured me it was not a problem. However, as we were outside, overlooking the water, enjoying the sunshine, the conversation was very cloudy.

Me, "Eric, can I get you anything?"

Eric, "No, thank you."

Me, "Would you like a drink?"

Eric, "No, thank you."

Me, "Are you okay?"

Eric, "Yes, thank you."

Me, "Well, what the hell?" (Just kidding, I didn't say that)

I began to feel a bit itchy. Was I getting a rash? And my stomach was starting to churn. Was I coming down with something? Yes! A bit of - `what the ...' - was my self-diagnosis.

In my usual fashion, I was hopeful and wanted to please. I suggested we go to my favorite place in the area, which is a sculpture/indoor/outdoor garden. I loved to spend hours there. So off we went. He seemed to enjoy it. *Seemed* to be the operative word here. He was quiet (shocker). I tried and tried to get some sort of reaction, comment, emotion, or even a 'fuck this' out of him. But there was not even a shadow of the Eric I had met in Sturgis.

I was a Rotary member at the time of his visit. The next day, I took him to our monthly meeting as my guest. My fellow Rotarians were a warm, welcoming group that I had known for many years. Some of us traveled abroad together to install water filters, donate school supplies, paint buildings in the barrio, etc. I thought that this group of wonderful people could loosen up Eric, if anyone could. No luck. He was awkwardly quiet and, quite frankly, embarrassing for me. Certainly, my fellow Rotarians must have wondered why I brought him along. At that point, I wondered too.

I kept asking him if he was okay. He said, "Yes," in his usual fluent manner. He was so distant for the short duration of his visit. There was no hugging, no kissing, no nothing! Barely a grunt.

Finally, it was time to go to the airport. (Whew)

When I got out to hug him goodbye, he hugged me so tight! I was shocked! When he finally stepped back, he had tears in his eyes.

He said, "I will miss you more than you'll ever know."

I guess that's right. His behavior certainly wasn't congruent with those words. I think I almost fell over when he said that. Good thing he was hanging on to me, or I'd have been on the pavement.

Eric never explained any of his behavior or words to me. So I'll never know. Once Eric got to my house, he clammed up and never poked his head out of that shell. No matter how many times I asked, he refused to tell me what was on his mind.

There was no talk of feelings, disappointment, expectations, appreciation, or musings of any sort. Then came the extremely sensitive and emotional comment as he was leaving. My mind-reading skills are null and void. It left me dumbfounded and confused!

What I do know: communication and conversation are crucial. We should have discussed in depth what a visit from one state to another would look like ahead of time. We should have made sure we were on the same page.

~~~~~

Coping idea -- How about tossing a salad on this one. Throw the ingredients up in the air and see if anything lands!!! Or, communication.
~~~~~

4

Don't Trust Too Soon or From Afar; Don't Be Duped

Richard

Richard was an online person who lived in Ohio, which meant he was about 5 hours away. Not an ideal situation, but being the Positive Polly that I am, I thought he could be "The One."

Richard and I spent many hours on the phone. We discussed his military background, his photojournalist background, his family, his daughters, and many other topics. Those conversations led us to believe we should meet in person. He lived in Ohio, and I in Michigan, but he agreed to drive my way, get a hotel, and be the perfect gentleman. YAY!

The day he was to arrive, I got a call saying, "I've hit a pothole with my jeep. It was so deep, my wheel is bent."

That must have been some black hole he hit. He's not going to make it to meet me. Duh!

He continued to call, and eventually the car was fixed. He'd like to come again. Uuummmmm. Reluctantly -- OK. On the day he was coming to see me, he was called by the TV station he worked for, and he needed to go to Europe. There was unrest in Brussels, and he was to leave immediately. Oh my gosh, it must be serious. He assured me he would be protected, but may not be able to call as often. I respond, "Of course not. Please be safe."

About five days later, he texted me. "My interviewer partner has died, and I have been injured."

I got that message in the middle of the night and didn't see it until morning because of the time difference. Oh my gosh, how awful. I was unable to reach him even though I tried and tried. For days, I wondered what happened.

A week later, I heard from him. He told me he was flown by helicopter to the military hospital in Germany, and he was awaiting the doctor's arrival. Oh my goodness!! I felt terrible for him. But what can I do? My responses were very kind and sympathetic. I was also sad since I thought we had a very special beginning.

A few days later, he told me he made it back to the States and was at Walter Reed National Military Medical Center in Bethesda, MD. I was pleased he was back in the States.

We had previously talked about his three daughters, who sounded delightful; they had been summoned. They were to arrive soon. They were summoned because he needed a very serious operation, and he may not make it. He was on heavy medication and awaiting test results. How horrible!

I even asked, "Would you like me to fly out there? Is there anything I can do?"

He assured me his daughters would keep me posted. He had told them about me. Awww, how nice.

A few hours later, his daughter, Christine, began texting me on HIS phone. She told me she had been reading the communication between her dad and me. She thought we had such a beautiful love story. She was excited to meet me. I responded that she was kind and that it would be a pleasure to meet when her dad was better. I also asked her to keep me posted on the surgery's outcome, his progress, etc.

Richard and his daughters kept me posted -- all on his phone, but explaining "This is Christine" or "This is Stephanie." Or just him.

Many days later, I got a call from Richard. He told me the operation was successful, but recovery would be slow, and he would be in the hospital for a few more days. Perhaps I should have asked more detailed questions regarding the surgery and recovery, but I thought he would share more if necessary.

In the course of this conversation regarding the surgery, hospital, daughters, etc. a little beep goes off in my head. And it was not a hospital monitor. A RED flag pops up. (*There's that red flag again.*) I don't recall the exact thing that was said, but I can tell you exactly where I was at that moment. I was driving to work on Burton Street, very close to Division. (*Our brains are amazing, aren't they?*)

Something wasn't right. I actually pulled over and stopped the car. A brilliant idea was triggered. Why not use that wonderful invention - social media - and do a little sleuthing? I did just that. I asked to be friends with his oldest daughter. She accepted my request almost immediately. I direct message her, "Hello, this is Scarlet, your Dad's friend. I'm checking to see how your Dad is doing. Remember, we were texting when he was at Walter Reed."

Her response was, "Who is this?" I reiterated who I was and about the above conversation. Her response, "I haven't spoken to my father in five years! He's a lying, manipulative, raging alcoholic!"

OMG!!!! How in the world did I get so "played" by Richard. I felt like such a fool. It was easy to prey on my sympathetic nature. I was drawn into the seriousness of his situation. But I was also furious! What kind of piece of shit goes to that extreme to dupe another human being? How can that bring satisfaction or pleasure of any kind to someone???

Since I'm not a liar, manipulator, narcissist or any of the other derogatory characteristics that would drive this type of person, it's a bit harder for me to see those traits in other people. However, the minute it becomes clear, watch out. I called him and blew him a new one across the airwaves. It was received with a hang-up on his end.

Apparently, he can dish it out but he can't take it.

Unfortunately, I deleted the messages and his voicemail, blocked him on my phone, and deleted all his information from every device I owned. I did all the "adult" (ha ha) things we sometimes do when we can't see straight because of our anger.

I actually wish I had some of those messages today, since I could look back on them. There are lessons of enlightenment and empowerment in all of these encounters. I wish I could review this guy. But, alas, I just moved on and have more stories to tell. Stay tuned.

~~~~~~

Coping -- There is no medal of honor here. I was suckered in.

How about a well-shaken martini and a dance party.

As Taylor Swift sang, "Shake it Off"
~~~~~~

5

When Someone Ghosts You, Respect The Dead and Move On

Josiah

Josiah's profile on Match.com was impressive. He was handsome, articulate, spoke about his family, and was a Naval Academy graduate who had been on the football team. The Naval Academy was a historical landmark and a large attraction in Annapolis. When I lived there, I toured the Academy several times and had great respect for the perseverance of its graduates.

Josiah and I had a few conversations on Match.com, then quickly moved on to exchanging cell numbers. He also gave me his Facebook profile and employer information. There are a number of fake profiles on websites, but I felt fairly confident he was legitimate because I could see his Facebook posts, and his current job site was right in Annapolis.

Our first date was lunch at Choptank, a nice restaurant in downtown Annapolis overlooking the bay. When he saw me, there was an immediate "Well, Hello!!" The hostess commented on my purple eyeshadow, and Josiah said I looked great. He, surprisingly, was as handsome as his photos. Once seated, we immediately began conversing. That was when I knocked over his water glass with my flailing hands. Fortunately, most of the water stayed on the table and didn't end up in his lap, but I was so embarrassed. Apparently, I was quite nervous, which is rare for me. I managed to calm down as the server cleaned up my mess, and Josiah, kindly, assured me it was no big deal.

We talked about our respective moves to the area, our families, our goals, and how attractive we found each other. He said many endearing things to me. And I admit, I'm a sucker for hearing nice things about myself. It's one of the things I didn't hear while growing up. I was vulnerable right out of the shoot.

After lunch, when he walked me to my car, he said, "You check all the boxes for me. I'm very attracted to you. Can we meet again?"

My response, "YES." I was excited.

We both had travel plans for a few days, but we kept in touch the entire time we were apart. We texted and talked often. Once we both returned, another lunch meeting at the same restaurant was planned. When there, our conversation was again very smooth and easy. He was charming, suave, polite, and again mentioned our attraction. I agreed wholeheartedly.

During that lunch, he said, "This is our special place. I will always think of this as _OUR_ restaurant.

Me, "Awwwww, really?"

He said, "Yes. That is how I am."

How nice. He was winning me over.

We agreed to meet again, this time on Saturday, which was three days away. We talked about dinner, golf, walking, or just hanging out. We didn't decide the time or place, just that Saturday was the day.

On Friday, around 5 p.m., I texted Josiah to ask if we could discuss the specifics for the next day. No big decision had to be made, but I wanted to know his thoughts on which activity, what time, and where. (What if I needed a new outfit?) I received a text back that said,

"I have had a long week. I'm just not up for having to plan anything…I'm shutting down for the weekend. I need a break. I'll reach out to you next week. If you're not interested, I get it and will simply extend you the best."

WHAT the … I didn't see that coming. What happened? Why the change in the blink of an eye? I asked myself if I had done something wrong. Two days later I sent a text asking if anything was seriously wrong and hoped things were fine. A *week* later, he sent a text saying I was "kind." That's it?!?!? Yes, I am kind, and sometimes too kind. I did not lose my cool, nor did I get angry. But a week or so later, I sent him a text saying,

"In the past two weeks, I have dealt with … (many disturbing things). Since you ghosted me and blocked me, it gave me plenty of time to reflect on my life and what is important to me. I have no room in my mind, body, and soul for anyone who would prey on one's emotions. You said you were honorable. Honesty would have been honorable. I won't waste my time on humans who are not kind, empathetic, respectful, and forthrightly honest."

I stated my thoughts and feelings about his actions and assumed that would be the end of that. It wasn't. He actually unblocked me, responded via text, called later in the day, and apologized. He said he wanted to see me again and apologize in person. He wasn't offended, agreed I was worthy of better behavior and that he had not acted responsibly. OMG, that's so rare. This guy was weaving his way back in.

I agreed to meet him. He invited me to his apartment, which was a first. Once I got there, he apologized, said many nice things and wanted us to continue seeing each other with the intention of being a monogamous couple. I melted.

We talked more about the future. I was a bit skittish since he had already bailed on me. However, I still believed we had an amazing connection. I knew he was very busy with work, but I thought I was a strong, independent woman and could handle that. I mentioned to him I was heading out of town on a short golfing trip with friends the following week. He offered to drive me to and from the airport even though it would be out of his way. That was a chivalrous offer. WOW! Perhaps second chances do work out. (*Keep in mind, I'm a romantic.*) I sent him my itinerary the next day so he could include that in his very busy calendar.

He told me he had to go to NYC for "family reasons" on the upcoming weekend, but would be back on Sunday and wanted to see me then. On Sunday afternoon, I received a text saying he wouldn't make it back and would call on Monday. He then blocked me before I could even respond. My gut did a flip. Guess what... no call. He blocked me for several days with no mention of his aforementioned offer to take me to and from the airport. My trip was coming up in a few days.

A few *weeks* later, he sent a text saying he wanted to see me.

I caved and agreed to see him.

At the last minute, he said he had forgotten about a work commitment he had, but would come after that. I told him not to bother, but he convinced me he wanted to come see me. He actually did show up, and we had a very lovely chat. He wanted us to be a forever item, and he said he would marry me. Previously, he had said he wasn't interested in marrying again. But now, he wants something serious. I'm such a sucker for a handsome face, and his was very handsome.

He mentioned he needed to go to Europe for work for a few days next week. The day he's leaving, he texts to say we shouldn't text during his trip and that he'll call when he returns.

He doesn't! Shocker!

Weeks later, I sent him a text saying, "Thank you for showing your true colors before we became entangled! Honorable, my ass."

He actually wrote back saying that wasn't how I truly felt and he wanted to see me. Oh sure. Block, unblock, ghost for weeks. I felt like a pinball. Since he had blocked me on Facebook, I couldn't see him on there either. But I have friends. One of them pulled up his profile and saw him with another woman at the Met when he was there for "family reasons."

That's enough for me. All those lovely words, my romantic beliefs, all my wishing and hoping couldn't change that tiger's stripes.

When someone's actions are very different than their words, believe the actions. That's where the proof is. The real character of a person is BEHAVIOR. He could look me in the eye and lie. I felt like a pinball being smacked around from bumper to bumper.

Am I like the pinball wizard…deaf, dumb, and blind? Yup, with that guy, I sure was. And he sure played a mean pinball!

People (men and women) can be so manipulative, self-absorbed, and narcissistic. They are smooth talkers and know how to prey on others. I've had both men and women treat me horribly. Be self-aware and protect yourself. Learn why you let people with these tendencies into your life. (*I know it sucks to know therapy might be needed.*)

Should you ghost people back? I think it's cowardly. If you claim to be honorable, live that way. Ghosting is deceptive in my opinion.

Here's the fun part. Keep the texts; you can always use them to write a book.

~~~~~

How about a Zombie cocktail for this guy? Enjoy!
~~~~~

6

Where's the Transparency?

Clint

As mentioned previously, I went to Sturgis for Bike Week a couple of times. Let's face it, for us Harley riding girls, Bike Week can be almost as romantic as Paris. Since I was working at my friend's pop-up store selling biker gear, not riding, I didn't have much free time. But for me, it was intoxicating just to be there. Since I loved all things motorcycle, this was exciting! I was part of the event!!!

One day, a couple of guys walked into the store. One was a tall, gangly guy, but the other reminded me of Clint Eastwood - -cowboy style. He had a lavender bandana around his neck, which I thought was adorable. Low and behold, they came over and talked to me. I have no recollection of what the conversation truly consisted of, but I know I sold a T-shirt or two. When they came back the next day, I was pleasantly surprised. This time, Cowboy Clint asked what time I got off work and if he could buy me a beer. Of course, I had to check since I was working, but my very sweet boss, Denny, said I could leave early.

That night the three of us went for a beer. Before the beer, they showed me their bikes, which were absolutely stunning. After the beer, Third Wheel Gangly Guy disappeared while Clint walked me home, holding my hand. It was comfortable and nice. The next day, he stopped by again, but I was leaving that day, which made me a bit sad. It had been such a great time. I gave Clint my business card, and he promised to call. And he did, about a week later. But that was fine. My expectations were low.

We continued talking on the phone, and before long, we were making plans for him to come to Michigan. Since he was from Montana and we both worked, it took a little planning, but we finally figured out a day and time. The day of his flight, there were mechanical and weather issues. Damn. But he finally made it, a number of hours later than expected, but he had arrived. I was excited.

We stopped and had a small bite to eat that night, but it was quite late.

The next day, we made up for lost time by driving into town to make a day of it. We went to the Grand Rapids Public Museum, which was delightful. We went into one of my favorite clothing boutiques. I saw a jacket I liked very much, and Clint was kind enough to buy it for me. We had a bite to eat and a very nice outing. There was no tension or awkwardness. That evening, we had dinner at the nicest restaurant in my little hometown. Then we went to the local pub where we ran into my best guy friend, John. He also had a Harley. John and I have often ridden together, so it was nice he was there and could meet Clint. It's always nice to have an opposite sex opinion; they got along nicely. If a date can meet a guy friend and not have a negative reaction, that's a plus.

Looking back, I'm wondering if there was too much wining and dining. Was he trying too hard to impress me? Hindsight is 20/20, right?

But while Clint was visiting, we discussed his living situation, why his mom was living with him, his small son, his older son out east, his goals, my goals, etc. It seemed we wanted many of the same things in life and enjoyed each other's company very much.

The next day, John, Clint, and I met at the Harley dealership for a BBQ they were hosting. It was a nice outdoor event. Since we all had "Harley" in common, it was fun. Then off to the airport and goodbye to Clint for this visit.

Things were going so well, we had made arrangements for me to go to Montana the next month to be together again, meet his family, and for me to see his environment. Once I was there, the introductions were made. It was obvious his young son was happy to meet me, and his mother genuinely liked me. That evening, we went out with his friends. On the back of his Harley, he showed me around Billings. All good stuff! We started making plans for the future…we would move to Jersey, he would work with his older son, who had a successful business, then he and I would retire in Belize. We'd have all our kids, our moms, a big happy family, and live happily ever after.

Sounds great, right? So idealistic! Retire in Belize!!! Oh my!

Unfortunately, a couple of weeks later, he called and told me some friends had posted some stupid stuff on his Facebook page that wasn't true. Questioning him a little further, I realized he was on his bike with his friend's girlfriend on the back. Right where I had been! Why? The explanation was that Troy (his friend) had a single seat on his bike. Clint had a double seat. So, Troy's girlfriend rode with Clint. When he had to stop quickly, he ran into the back of a car. Both of them had to jump off quickly! OMG! I didn't have time to get the whole story, but I made sure everyone was OK. I had arrived at my mom's house, where I was to have dinner with her and my daughter. We would have to talk later.

Of course, the first thing I did when I got back home was look at his Facebook page and see what was posted. It wasn't funny, and "the girlfriend" said she had ended up in the hospital from the accident. We were to "pray" for her. What the…?

I had tried and tried to call. No answer. Clint finally called a day or so later; he realized I was quite upset. I was calmed by his explanation.

But, the seed of doubt was planted.

The following Saturday, I tried to reach him on his cell many times. I wasn't calling to check up on him, but I needed help with my hot water heater. The pilot light had gone out. Since he is very mechanically inclined, I wanted him to walk me through the lighting process, so I didn't blow up my house or have to pay $100 for a house call. I called the house and got his mother. I asked her why I could not reach Clint on his cell phone.

"Well, you know where he is don't you?" she asked.

"No, I thought he might be at home with his cell phone off," I responded.

"He's with Rebecca," she said.

"Troy's girlfriend?" I asked.

"She's not Troy's girlfriend", she said. "She was here Sunday and then Thursday night until 2 a.m. I told Clint he had to take her home. Then last night he came home from work, packed a bag, and left the house."

Oh My God. He was with Rebecca. Clint's mother also told me the house was really hers, not his. He had no money and he paid her half of the mortgage, not the other way around. He had to live there financially, and Grandma took care of his son more often than not. Wow, what a kick in the gut for me. I believed his lies.

So, in my very calm, thoughtful way (ha ha), I started to drink a bottle of wine which led to calling my mother, sobbing. I ended up going to her house and spent the night. Clint finally called on Sunday night, 24 hours later. He told me his mother didn't know her own name. Too late. I no longer believed anything he said and my dreams of our life together were crushed. Again, my calm, thoughtful self (sarcastic), sent text messages and voicemails that HE didn't answer, but Rebecca did!!! Are you kidding me??? She boldly told me Clint was with her now and always would be!

"Well, you can have him sista!"

He's an ass for being a liar and a coward for not having the gonads to tell me himself! YUK!

Almost a year later, I got a letter of apology. I am not sure if he really wrote it or if his mother did. Either way, I sent it back!

Ta ta Cowboy Clint. No one deserves to be treated that way.

~~~~~

Coping idea -- Hop on your Harley and ride!!! Let the wind in your face be your HIGH. No cocktail needed!
~~~~~

Jacob

An internet connection. (*Can we please find other options, but what?*). From his emails, pictures, and conversations, he seemed like a good guy. Who doesn't love a guy who posts a picture of himself with his dog, right?

He lived about two hours away, which could be a challenge. But I've never shied away from a challenge! A number of conversations took place via the phone, which led me to believe he was intelligent, interesting, and a gentleman. He lived in a lovely part of Michigan on the Grand Traverse Bay, so I knew he wasn't homeless or living in a tent. Within a few weeks, he invited me to visit. He would buy lunch if I did the drive. It's a long way to go for lunch, but it was summertime in Michigan. What's not to love? He had a main house and a guest house in case an overnight was needed, and I was up for an adventure. I alerted family and friends as to the location and agreed to drive to his neck of the woods. Let the games begin.

We met at a restaurant -- a public place -- in case I needed to bail or it just seemed wrong.

As soon as we sat down for lunch, he told me his divorce was five years ago. That was the year he had a stroke and his wife decided she wasn't cut out to be a caregiver. Yikes! That's a lot!

"She is a high-powered executive," he said. He then

proceeded to tell me her position, with what company, etc. He obviously was quite proud of her, and perhaps not entirely over the pain that she had caused him. I felt bad for him, and it touched my heart. I couldn't help but wonder, "Who leaves their husband during his time of crisis?" Maybe I should have been asking myself what's the rest of the story? What was my gut telling me?

Regardless of the stroke, we had a very nice time and did some fun things. I rode his motorcycle, took a tour of the surrounding area, drove his fast car, etc. He had nice things and the dog was very cute and friendly. Signs of a stroke were minimal.

Once I got back to work, co-workers were asking about my trek to the Bay. Lo and behold, one person knew him from her high school days and had a crush on him back then. OMG, this world is way too small!

Apparently, his family was much more influential than he had let on. My coworker said many nice things about him and his family. They were apparently well-respected in the community, which reassured me. A bit of background helps with trust.

A few days went by, then he phoned and wanted me to come up again. He explained it was difficult for him to drive long distances since the stroke. He asked if I would drive to his place again. Since he had filled my gas tank and been a gentleman last time, I agreed to go. Again, a good time was had by all.

We continued to see each other for a few months. Things were going well. There was, however, a comment when we were going over to his friend's place. He said, "Maybe you'll like him more than me."

My reaction, "What? Why would you say that?"

Jacob, "Always good to have Plan B."

Me, "OH really?" (Does he have Plan B?) Hmmmm? My gut did a little flip!

There were also a number of times I couldn't reach him. He had given me his landline and cell numbers, but he often didn't get back to me for hours…sometimes days. But in my true naivety, I let it slide…except in my gut.

As we approached the holiday season, he said he was coming my direction because he had family in the area. (Well, isn't that nice -- now driving my way wasn't an issue). Additionally, he wants to know what I'd like for a gift. I'm a bit surprised by all of this and told him that it was totally unnecessary. He insisted.

Since we had listened to a lot of music when we were together, he suggested that he give me his old phone with over

5,000 songs on it. We would just have to switch sim cards, and all should be fine. That sounded reasonable and acceptable. We agreed on that.

Done. EXCEPT, the day we did this, his emails kept coming in along with the music. An email arrived as I was on my way to work, which was from Carol. I was at a red light and decided to look at it. "Jacob, thank you so much for the wonderful dinner and spending the night with me last night. It meant so much to me, and you have inspired me to lose the 60 pounds I have gained."

What????? He spent the night with someone 60 pounds overweight the night before he came to see me?? I wondered why he was at my house by 11 a.m. -- before his proposed arrival. He had told me he rarely got up before 10 a.m. He wasn't excited to see ME; he was excited to leave the one-night stand! What the…?

Talk about hurt! I had asked him about other women in prior conversations, but apparently didn't get an honest answer. We were planning a trip together, and he had talked about the following summer and the fun we would have. How could I have been so blind? Or was he just a good liar? I had even shared my previous deceitful relationship with him. He told me I didn't deserve to be treated like that. But he was traveling around the state "meeting and greeting" many others in the few months that I had known him.

I pulled the car over. I was so angry. I called him immediately. He stammered a bit, but at my insistence, agreed to meet me to explain. I called work, said I'd be late, and met Jacob at a coffee shop. The details are blurry (literally because of all the tears), but the truth came out. He had actually traveled to the other side of the state to meet Carol the night before. He spent the night there and then came to see me. YUK. Enough!

Was he trying to prove something because of his stroke? Was his hurt by his wife, causing him to take it out on other women? Was he just an asshole? Should I have asked more questions, or been concerned about the red flags that my gut was showing me? I was confused and hurt. I'll never know for sure who or what he is truly about. What I do know is "Trust Your Gut." I had a funny feeling, but couldn't nail it. I was swayed by his wonderful lifestyle, charm, personality, and others' knowledge who had known him prior to his stroke and divorce. A woman's intuition is far more accurate than any other aspect of a relationship. None of those things was worth the deceit I felt. I felt raw and crushed. I should have listened much more closely to ME!!!

~~~~~

Coping idea -- Ahi tuna with some *damn it* hot sauce is in order. And maybe a Lemon Crush for the bitter taste left in my mouth, and gut!

Here's a good tune to play: Sam Smith - I'm not the Only One
~~~~~

Jo's Journey

7

Too Much Too Soon

Kyle

Kyle and I met online. That seems to be the way of the world. As it turned out, however, he lived 10 minutes from me. (I could have saved the subscription fee to Match.com.) When he sent me an email, I looked at his pictures and thought, "Why do I recognize this guy?" Then it hit me. I've seen him at The Pub, a local bar and grille that my friends and I frequent. The Pub offers happy hour promotions for motorcycle enthusiasts. Since I had that beautiful lava red Harley Davidson Softail Deluxe named Mariah, I loved this place. Outside, you could watch the sunset overlooking water (a former gravel pit), put your toes in the sand (brought in from landscapers), look at the palm trees (imported from Florida), and listen and/or dance to local bands. Yes, it's corny, but what's not to love?

I asked Kyle if he hung out there. Sure enough! I started asking around, and, yes, he was the one I thought. He was always in a baseball cap, with a casual attitude, and was frequently with a woman. And, he had a motorcycle. Yep, that's Kyle.

We started communicating, first through the dating site and then we exchanged phone numbers. Shortly thereafter, my girlfriend and I were on our way to a near-by beach town. Kyle happened to call while we were in the car. He told me he was on his boat in Grand Haven - which was where we were headed. He wanted us to meet him at his boat. That's not what I wanted to do on a first meeting, and I was with my girlfriend. I tell him my girlfriend and I are going to have a burger and a beer at a popular place in the area. He asked if he could join us. I checked with my friend, and she didn't mind. (What a good friend.)

I tell him, "It's fine if you want to join us for *a* beer."

He said, "Great, I'll stay for one beer. Then you girls can have the rest of the night to yourselves."

Sounds good, right? Wrong. He stayed for a <u>few</u> beers, even while we ate dinner. Then he wanted to buy us another one at a different place. My poor girlfriend. I tried to keep her in the conversation, but it was clear that Kyle wanted my attention. I felt like a bad friend. My girlfriend assured me she was fine. Even though things didn't go exactly as planned, we had a nice time. Kyle had come on a bit strong, but it actually felt good to meet a man who was so intensely interested. And it gave my friend and me a lot to talk about on our drive home.

We were not back home before Kyle dialed me up. He asked me to join him on his boat in a couple of days, just the two of us. I agreed. His boat was large enough to go out on Lake Michigan, so that would be cool. (Being on the water is my happy place.)

It was an absolutely gorgeous day when Kyle and I headed to the boat. We boarded the boat, headed through the channel, out to Lake Michigan, and anchored the boat. The sun glistened off the water. He had floats to lounge on with beer in hand. We could swim in the crystal-clear water. How fantastic. It was truly relaxing and enjoyable. I lived on inland lakes most of my adult life, but it was great to be on the "big lake." We had a wonderful time. Eager as ever, Kyle implored me to stay on the boat with him that night.

"No, no, no," I reply. Too much too soon.

He says, "Okay, but I'd like to see you again soon."

Our next date went swimmingly as well. Kyle seemed very intent on getting to know me. No playing it cool or waiting two weeks (or six months) to call again with this guy. He was into me and wasn't afraid to show it.

A couple of days later, he left on a family vacation for a few days. I was happy for him and wished him tons of fun. He sent a text once he arrived with a picture of where he was. He signed off with a hug and kiss, his usual sign off. What I thought was unusual: five other people were included in the text. Do all his contacts get a hug and a kiss? Thinking he had done this by mistake, I texted him immediately and told him he had sent it to me and five others. He called right away and said I shouldn't be concerned about that. He typically signs off that way.

Oh! I thought I was special…how silly of me. I asked him if any of the people in the text were his old girlfriends that he had told me he kept in contact with. Sure enough, that was the case. Well! So much for that undivided attention that I thought was just for me. But I told myself that it was no big deal. He had been honest, and we had only known each other a short time. That's Kyle.

Once he returned from his family outing, we agreed to meet at The Pub on bike night. When I walked in, there happened to be about eight other people there that I knew. In my usual friendly manner, I stopped to have a quick chat with each of them before I made my way to Kyle. He greeted me with a flip comment about it being his turn. I laughed but made a note to myself. Suddenly, this confident, carefree guy with multiple girlfriends seems a bit snarky. Within a matter of minutes, he was playing Dr. Freud. He matter-of-factly informed me that I had commitment issues. He then went on to tell me I would never find love if I didn't let my guard down. What? I've known this guy for about four weeks, and he was telling me what he thinks my issues are!?!?!?

Don't get me wrong. I have my hang-ups and flaws just like everyone else, but being "commitment phobic" is not one of them. I put myself out there looking for Mr. Right For Me. Apparently, I found Mr. Pay Attention to Only Me. Even though that wasn't what he was doing in return. Wasn't he the one sending messages to multiple people with hugs and kisses? Hmmmm.

He's the one who has gotten ultimatums from girlfriends because he wouldn't commit, not me. Those were not my issues, but since Kyle wasn't getting what Kyle wanted, he tried very hard to put this situation in my basket.

I cooled off my responses to him. We had more discussions about previous relationships. I realized he was quite needy. He wanted a woman around very badly, but couldn't let go of the former girlfriends.

Needless to say, I took a giant step back.

Women are often characterized as being "in love with being in love", desperate to find a mate. There are also many men who suffer from those same issues. Many people feed off that energy and can form codependent relationships. I have fallen into that trap. After my divorce, I had to LEARN the hard way (with much professional therapy and many uncomfortable dates) to be alone and okay.

I was married for many years. If you've been in that situation, you know when you are a wife and mother, your privacy and solo time (even in the bathroom) go right out the window. It's a very difficult transition, but I began the journey of finding Scarlet again. I had to face her directly and attempt to love her again. When I stepped back from Kyle (regardless of all the attention), I began to enjoy an evening on the couch with a good book and a glass of wine ~ all by myself!!!

Who knew?

47

~~~~~

Listen to Miley Cyrus Grammy winning song, "Flowers." It's a great message.
~~~~~

8

What Puzzle Piece Fits Where?

Ryan

Ryan was like a jigsaw puzzle. He described himself as 5'10"; in reality, he was closer to 5'7". His skin seemed too big for his body; he looked like a 50-year-old infant. His voice was low - like an easy listening tone. His demeanor was calm, yet his world was full of scattered pieces that hadn't been connected.

Our first meeting was at a coffee shop. It was brief but the conversation was interesting and flowed easily. He had a great smile and a warm spirit. When he walked me to my car, he asked if he could contact me again. I said that would be fine. So he did … about *six months later*.

He apologized for the six month wait when he called and asked me to dinner. I agreed to meet him. I've never been one to hold grudges, and I was curious about his life. During dinner, he began to explain the reasons for the long space of time between phone calls. One, his business had lost a major client. They needed to revamp the entire operation to compensate for the loss. That's a major client.

Two, he was just coming out of a relationship. He could have mentioned THAT at coffee, but why be upfront? Because of those two issues, he thought it was better to wait. He said he was now ready to come up for air and pursue a relationship.

Since dinner had gone well, I agreed to see him again the following week. This time I was going to bring along a few friends to get a second opinion. He passed the "friend test," and we soon started spending more time together.

Within a few weeks, he asked me if I would like to meet his five-year-old daughter. Yes, he had adopted a five year old daughter when he was in his 50's. It was faster than I would have moved things with my own kids, but my children were beyond the young phase. So, it was his call. Things were going well with us, and I was happy to meet the little one. He also introduced me to his other babies...the two giant black labradors that I affectionately referred to as the "damn dogs." The introductions were complete. Soon after that, I received an invitation to his daughter's sixth birthday party. I would also be meeting his much younger ex-wife at the party. Lucky, lucky me. One big happy family.

Over the next few months, Ryan and I continued to spend time together, mostly on days he didn't have his daughter. Since he and his ex had joint custody, he had his daughter quite frequently. They also shared custody of the two dogs, which was a new one for me.

With his business still struggling to recover, things were a little tight for him financially, so I kicked in for dates most of the time. I'm a bit old-fashioned in this regard and don't usually pay for dates. Ryan, however, assured me it was temporary. His business would recover soon because a new partner was involved. During one of our conversations about the business, I learned there were three other partners, one being his ex-wife. Yup, every day he was at work, he was with his ex-wife. Ever the people pleaser, I worked hard to convince myself that this was no big deal. However, there was a part of me that really wasn't happy about how much his current life was still intertwined with his ex-wife.

One day, I was talking to a coworker/friend about Ryan. Turned out she knew him. Her comment to me was, "He's such a nice guy. If you can't make it work with him, it must be you!" That was a rather disconcerting comment. And, I thought a rather mean thing to say if I were her *friend!* Was she judging my dating experiences? What was she saying about me? I tried, however, to focus on the "he's so nice part." More than one thing came to my mind at that moment; however, that made Ryan not quite the perfect specimen this "friend" seemed to think.

For one thing, he treated his dogs like they were just as much his children as his daughter...and his responsibilities to them always came before my needs and desires. Dates were cut short for him to leave because of the dogs. Was I less important than the dogs? In addition, his duties to his damn dogs and young daughter were often unpredictable. With all this shared custody of both his daughter and the dogs, arrangements were constantly changing at the last minute, disrupting our plans. When his ex-wife got some last-minute tickets to the symphony, Ryan agreed to take the kids (his daughter and dogs), and we were a no-show at the dinner party we had planned to attend. God forbid he say no to his ex.

Additionally, I always seemed to come last on his list of priorities. Obviously, it made perfect sense for a father to put the needs of his child over a woman with whom he was in the early stages of dating. There were, however, a few occasions when it was important to me to have him with me for an event. There were times he refused to even TRY to get a babysitter. UGH.

Don't get me wrong, Ryan was, as our mutual friend had pointed out, a very nice man. He was courteous, calm, and polite. Even if our plans changed and we ended up eating pizza on the couch instead of a dinner party with friends, we had a great time together. His daughter was very sweet; it was endearing to see him interact with her and see his commitment as a father despite splitting time with his ex. My own children were a major priority in my life while growing up, so I was patient. I soon realized our relationship had an ever-changing schedule. I tried to tell myself it was just scattered pieces trying to connect. However, I was bubbling underneath the surface because my needs and wishes were being disregarded. Was I able to fit into this puzzle?

While dating Ryan, I had begun to rent my house. It was a nice money maker for me. My property was on a beautiful little lake. Since I spent a lot of weekends away with friends and family during the summer months, I figured, why not rent it to vacationers and make a little extra money instead of letting the beautiful house stay empty?

One weekend, when I had renters, Ryan offered to let me stay at his house. We had plans to see friends of his over the holiday weekend. Since my place was in hot demand, I figured it would be a good opportunity. As the time approached, however, he timidly informed me he could not afford to go out of town for the weekend. WELL...hmm, maybe his business wasn't doing so well.

He suggested this option, "In lieu of visiting friends this weekend, why don't my daughter and I spend time at your home? We can enjoy the lake and all it has to offer."

Wait! What? The house I just rented out?!?!?!?

I'd have to say no to my potential renters and refuse that extra cash that always came in handy. That pesky little people pleaser in me resurfaced again. I agreed to the weekend at my place. I had already arranged to take Saturday off work, and the weather was supposed to be beautiful. I would invite a few more friends over to make the most of things. I cancelled the renters.

The things we do for love.

The Wednesday before the weekend, Ryan and I had an evening alone, but he couldn't seem to shift his focus from his cell phone. When I asked who he was texting so attentively, he told me he was arguing with his ex about the dogs.

"She wants me to take the dogs this weekend," Ryan said.

"But she was taking them since we were going to Betty and Lou's." I replied.

"I know, but since we're not going now, it's really my weekend. But, I'm saying no."

The next night, I asked him about the dogs.

"Oh, I have them for the weekend. She would have to board them, so I said I'd take them."

"WHAT???"

"It's no big deal."

Like hell.

I love animals, but the "damn dogs" were not a good fit at my house. They were accustomed to running freely in Roger's large, fenced-in backyard, whereas my yard had no fences. That meant I would have the equivalent of two miniature horses running around my house like it was their own personal race track. I also knew my fifteen-year-old cat would not be keen on befriending those two giants. My lovely cat was too old to defend herself as she would have in her younger days.

Ryan and I had discussed the dog situation in the past, so imagine my surprise when he assumed the dogs were welcome at my place. I called on Friday morning to finalize the weekend arrangements. With no hint of apology, he casually said that he, his daughter, and the dogs would still come for the weekend.

I found myself needing to be the bad guy, a role I never enjoy playing! Even though we had been over this on more than one occasion, I had to get tough with him; bottom line - no dogs at my house. Board them, get a sitter for them, or how about telling your ex-wife no. I certainly lost more money than his ex would pay to board the dogs!!! What is wrong with this puzzle? Were the pieces fitting?

On another occasion, Ryan had wanted us to ride our respective Harleys for the day. His wife had the daughter and the dogs, so we could go for a nice, long ride. I agreed to meet him at the park in 45 minutes. We met up and headed out. My bike was not purring like normal, so I signaled Ryan to pull over at a gas station. We filled up, and I told him I wanted to go to the Harley dealership and get Mariah looked at.

He said, "I just checked in with the ex, and I have to get back."

"What?" I practically screamed.

Yup, he was heading back.

My volcano erupted.

All of that combined, I was not interested in fighting for a man who treated my time, money, patience, and effort as less valuable than his. He allowed his ex-wife to dictate his every move with no regard for how it affected MY life.

Although I've made a lot of progress, I still have some bad habits left over from my past. Occasionally, I still put the needs and wants of others over my own. Every good relationship requires compromise, but it's all too easy for me to cross the line into being so accommodating that I allow myself to be treated unfairly. I have to try very hard not to give way to the part of Scarlet that will say, "Well, it's not the way I want to do things, but sure, whatever you want."

I need to be regarded as an important part of the relationship, not the lowest priority.

~~~~~

Listen to YOUR heart. Be part of the big puzzle of a relationship that works for you. Get out a 1000 piece puzzle and make sure you're not piece 999 of 1000.
~~~~~

9

Fool Me Once, Shame On You; Fool Me Twice, Shame On Me

Peter

Peter was another internet connection. He lived in Ohio, but within a drivable distance. We talked about his thriving business, and my four part-time jobs. It was difficult to make a plan for a two-day date. But the Wonder Woman I was, I figured it out. Peter was coming up on Saturday. I managed to have that day off and the following morning.

For a first meet-and-greet, he would need to book a hotel, but a man in his fifties can certainly afford a one-night stay at an economical hotel. I gave him information on two hotels in the area. Both would accommodate his motorcycle trailer for hauling his bike. We planned to take a long ride on Saturday.

On Friday, I was headed to Human Resources for one of my jobs. That job wasn't going great, so I was happy to have a long ride on Mariah the next day. On my way to HR, I heard my text notification. Better check. It could be HR! Nope! It was Peter. He had bent the wheel of his bike while loading it onto the trailer. That was all the message said. Immediately, I attempted to call him and relay my sympathies regarding this horrific incident. He didn't pick up. Weird! I had JUST gotten the message!

After my visit to HR (which didn't go great), I got another text saying he was too angry to talk right now. Seriously!!! He's supposed to be arriving the next morning, but he's too angry to talk! I tried again. No answer. I waited, and waited, and waited. The next day, still waiting...nothing. Needless to say, he doesn't arrive and he doesn't call with any other explanation. Not a great weekend for Ms. Scarlet!!!

Months go by; yes, literally, MONTHS. Then a text. I have deleted his name from my phone, so I ask, "Who is this?" He says something to the effect, " Boy, you really did delete me."

DUH!

He tells me, "It's Peter...how have you been?"

Me, "Fine."

Chatter, chatter, chatter. Then, he brought up a visit to Michigan again. I reiterate the happenings of the former planned visit. He assured me that it would not happen again. He said to me, "Because you didn't believe me, I haven't contacted you." Oh, Yes. It must have been me who was at fault. Deflection - such an irritating characteristic.

More conversations took place. Finally, ever so hesitantly, I agreed to have him come to Michigan. We figured out a Saturday after work. He will get a hotel close by, we will have dinner, no strings attached, and all will be fine. Just the opportunity to finally meet. We talked on Friday. He will call me in the morning with his estimated time of arrival.

Uh huh! Do you think he called? NOPE! No call in the morning. Finally, I called him around noon. Guess what, he doesn't pick up. He sent a text saying he's at a car dealership and will call as soon as he gets finished making a deal. What? Is he buying a car on the day he's supposed to be coming to see me? Seriously? Surprise. No call. No show.

Sunday, I go on about my day. I went out to lunch, took a drive, and got to thinking. My spinning mind had a thought. We tried to meet twice now, hmmmmm. I called him. No answer. SHOCKER. I leave a voicemail saying, "Since you couldn't make it to Michigan, I'm on my way to Ohio to see you." This is the IMMEDIATE response I got:

" If I were doing what you are doing now, driving to my house unannounced, saying I was going to show up at your house, what would you do? Call the police, right? What you're doing is crazy. I just got off the phone with my local police department. I told them what you are doing. They are going to patrol my house two to three times an hour until I get home tomorrow. If you are on my property/driveway, etc., you will be arrested. Please turn around, go home, and call me tomorrow...am I perfectly clear?"

I laughed and laughed. I was lying on my couch when I made that call. I had no idea where he lived, and NO, I never would have done that. Ever! What an ass!

But alas, a few months go by. He contacted me again. What is with this guy?? He sends a few messages. I ignore them. Then he tells me he's coming to Michigan for a motorcycle rally and invites me to ride too. Are you kidding me? I can't. I'm working.

"Well, that's a shame," he says.

Ha ha, shame. Shame on me if I believed him. He wouldn't really be there anyway, I'm sure.

He then sends pictures of himself in Indianapolis.

I reply, "I guess you didn't come to Michigan again after all."

He writes back, "Do you want me to????" I can't believe it. I tell him he stood me up twice; there won't be a third time.

" Fine", he says. "Goodbye."

So long, farewell, adieu. Bye bye, Peter.

Fool me once - shame on you. Fool me twice, shame on

Scarlet Jo Hanson

me!!! But he wanted a third time. What the…

<div style="text-align: center">~~~~~</div>

Listen to: "Ex's and oh's" by Elle King

Samuel

I had recently moved to an unfamiliar area when a new friend invited me to a holiday gathering. I was thrilled. I was excited since I didn't know many people, and this would be a great opportunity to meet others. Also, she was a married woman. Often single people don't get invited to do things with couples. It's one of the "fall outs" of divorce. Therefore, I was doubly pleased about the invitation.

Once at their home, introductions were made with the other guests - single and coupled. Everyone brought abundant amounts of food, carols were being played in the background, and guests were mingling in a warm and friendly manner.

The hostess originated from another country, as did many of the guests. I loved that! It's always interesting to learn about other nationalities. Their perspective of the U.S. is fascinating to me.

Soon I realized one of the very handsome male guests was paying quite a bit of attention to me. We engaged in conversation, and I soon realized he was from France. We talked about Paris, I tried to recall my high school French - we both laughed at that! Oui, Oui.

We conversed about travel. Both of us had been to similar countries in the past. He also showed me some of his pictures from India and Japan; two places I would love to visit. He was very engaging. When it was time to eat, he sat next to me, offered to get me coffee, how would I like my coffee, and could he get me anything else? My goodness, what a gentleman. After he brought me coffee, he told me he had to leave soon. He had another engagement that evening. Before he left, he asked for my number. Since I knew the hostess and he had been so thoughtful, I believed it was fine to give him my number. He then handed me his business card which I simply slid into my jeans pocket and thanked him. Note to self -- remember to take that out of your pocket before you wash your jeans.

I stayed longer at the very enjoyable party - there was much talking and singing with the remaining guests. The host brought out his guitar, we sang, laughed, and had a great time. All too soon, it was time for me to leave.

Later that evening, I fished the business card out from my jean's pocket and set it on the counter (don't want the washer to eat it). A few minutes later, I got a text message from an unknown number. Could it be him? Maybe I better check. I looked closely at the card since the text had asked me to coffee the next morning. WHAT? He's the Ambassador to France? Holy Moly! No wonder he was so charming.

I can't go to coffee the next morning because I work from 11:00 a.m. to 6:00 p.m. that day. I explained that to him in a return text. He replied that he would be willing to take me to dinner after work instead.

Isn't that lovely? He's willing to drive 45 minutes to take me to dinner. He must be interested!

The next evening, just before closing time, it poured rain. Not to worry. Ambassador had sent a text saying he would pick me up at my work door. We will then drive together to the restaurant rather than meet there. Well, of course, I agreed to that. I locked the store door at exactly 6:00 and he was there waiting for me. But not just waiting, he had an umbrella and a bouquet of flowers. How very chivalrous. I'm not used to this type of behavior. YES, I'm impressed. We had a lovely dinner. The conversation flowed easily, he continued to be his charming self, and drove me back to my car. I was a bit fluttery inside. WOW!

The next day, text messages started rolling in, phone calls became frequent, and I found myself smiling about what a gentleman he was. During his lunch period, he would often text just to say something like "enjoy your lunch." Every day I received multiple kind, endearing messages and calls.

We continued to see each other often. We enjoyed so many things together - meals, museums, walks, and just drinking tea at his house while chatting. One Saturday night after dinner, we went back to his place. Over a cup of tea and a number of kisses, he said, "We should go on Holiday together. Let's plan something."

I'm like "SURE!"

We talk a bit more, but it was getting late. Time to go since I had that work thing again the next morning. He walked me to my car, kissed me good night (many times) and asked me to be sure to text when I arrived home. Of course, I did that, and he wished me a good night.

He was extremely endearing and his charm and chivalry were so impressive. His kindness and consideration made me melt.

The next morning I enjoyed my coffee and was awaiting my usual "Good morning" text. I left for work and still no text. Hmmmmm. Weird. Oh well. Hi ho, hi ho, it's off to work I go. By 11:30 I still hadn't heard, so I sent a text. He apologized and said he hadn't slept well. Okay. Later in the afternoon, more silence. Again, I reached out. He said he had been working since he had a busy week coming up. That made sense; he is a diplomat after all. I didn't get too wigged out. But by 8 o'clock that evening I knew in my gut something was wrong. I asked him to call me. I didn't hear back. By 9:30 p.m., I AM wigged out.

Had this been typical behavior, it would not have been so

bothersome. But since there had been multiple texts on a daily basis, I wondered what the heck happened. He had never used work as a reason to not communicate, and he wasn't even at work. Even when he had attended events, he would send a text or two. This behavior was most unusual. Therefore, I sent another text, "I don't deserve this silence for no reason. Last night we were talking about going on holiday. What has changed?"

He said he'd call in 10 minutes. And he did. He told me he was getting very attached to me. (Nice). He had such a hard time with his divorce and his relationship with his son because of the divorce, he didn't want to go through that pain again. Since he had to move back to France in a few years, he didn't want to get attached to me. He said,

"You won't move to France because your family is here."

" WHAT?" I respond. "I am a grown ass woman, why would you NOT discuss this before making that decision for me. Besides, that would be two years down the road, and YOU don't know that I won't go. My kids are grown and gone and living their own best lives."

But, alas, there is no hearing my point of view. He said goodbye.

Don't stop reading. That's not the end of this story.

After the above debacle and a couple months had passed,

I was having a conversation with my daughter. She invited me to visit her and her husband at their home in Amsterdam. Of course, that's a "Hell, YES!" She mentioned the dates, and, of course, I'll make that work! She then suggested I take the train from Amsterdam to Paris for a few days after I'm with them for a week; perhaps ask a friend to meet me there. (She knows nothing about the Ambassador.) I say, "Yes, what a great idea." I start making plans. I asked a few of my great travel girlfriends, but none could go during the time frame I needed. Oh well. I decided I'm going to go to Paris by myself. I can, as my therapist mentioned, "Fall in love with yourself in Paris." Great idea.

I started making plans with books and the internet. Another thought strikes - why not put on your big girl panties and ask Ambassador for advice and options? So I did. To my surprise, he very quickly responded back, asked me questions about my objectives for the trip, and said he was happy to help. I was surprised but was comfortable texting back and forth for a few weeks about the plans I eventually made. It was all very business-like, but I appreciated the help. I would spend time with my daughter and her husband in Amsterdam, then train to Paris for five nights like a single local.

(Yes, that is hard for me, but I no longer stop doing things just because I need to go alone.)

OKAY. Ready, set, go. A friend of mine will drop me at

Dulles Airport for my flight to Amsterdam. She is very kind to do that. Drinks and apps upon my return for her kindness. She dropped me at the door of my airline, I head inside and turn left and head that direction; nope, wrong way. Then I turn right to head the other way. Coming through the very door I just walked through one minute ago is none other than Ambassador. *SERENDIPITY, THE UNIVERSE, THE ODDS!!*

We looked intently at each other, walked immediately toward each other and then embraced in a very long, intense hug that felt like home. Immediately, he started complimenting me. We chatted briefly about my trip, talked about where he was going, etc. Then he asked me to wait for him while he got his boarding pass and visa. It took him quite a few minutes. So, I jokingly said to him. "Are you changing your flight to join me in Paris?" He chuckled and said he wished he could, but no. Then we head to security.

He offered to carry my bags, kissed the top of my head as we went through security, and held my one empty hand as we headed to the inner airport train to our respective terminals. I am on cloud nine thinking the Universe has intervened by bringing us back together. He agreed. As we boarded the inner airport train to get to our respective terminals, we were linked together as if we were Siamese twins. Once we reached his terminal, which was before mine, he kissed me goodbye, stepped off the train and turned back to look at me until the train started to move again and he was no longer visible. I entered the dark tunnel headed to my terminal with tears in my eyes. DAMN.

Once at my gate, I checked my phone. Sure enough, he had texted to say how great it was to see me. Ditto. Then I tell him, "It's my lucky day because I got to see you and I just got upgraded to first class." (My daughter does that for me at times - love her!) He responds to me saying, "Ditto, he saw me and he was upgraded." I didn't need an airplane. I was flying high.

All during my trip, he sent texts. "If you need anything at all, just call. Any time," he said.

My trip was great. No issues. Not the best way to fall in love with myself since he was my back-up the entire time. I didn't care. I was so relaxed and happy.

He wanted to see me upon my return home. I agreed, but with the caveat that we needed to discuss the previous 'run away'. He agreed. He came to my place the night after I returned home. We had dinner and talked all about what happened. He told me more about his family breakup and apologized for his poor behavior last time. He told me it wouldn't happen again! His loving, kind, compassionate and passionate words and behavior seemed genuine. All was well. He wanted to come again the next evening.The next evening, Friday, traffic was particularly difficult heading my direction. His original E.T.A. was 90 minutes. Then it was delayed to about twice as long. But I patiently awaited his arrival.

He eventually arrived, and we had another lovely evening. Things were going so well, I invited him to join me and my family for Easter brunch which was the upcoming Sunday. He said, "Sure."

He left quite late that evening, but traffic was fine. The trip home was the usual 45 minutes when he sent a text telling me he was home safe.

The next day I sent a text. "Since you've driven my way the last two times, why don't I meet you at your place after my Easter brunch with the kids? I'm so excited we are back together."

He responded, "After spending so much time in traffic, I realize how difficult it would be for us to see each other often as we live far apart. A long-distance relationship cannot be sustainable. I don't think either of us would accept seeing each other only on weekends or once in a while. That's not what either one of us is looking for. So sorry about that."

OMG, I thought I had found my LOVE! But NO!

Who is this person -- he thinks he is the singular sensation who makes all the decisions. That is twice now that he has done that. Wouldn't it be appropriate and generally speaking, just considerate, to discuss these things. And certainly not in a text message.

I was so very angry. That seemed extremely opposite of the way he was conversing and behaving. I was blindsided again. Then he would not talk to me again. No texts, no nothing.

I should have believed his actions the first time. He had told me he didn't believe in hurting others for one's own self. Ha ha. Isn't that what he just did to me. His actions spoke much louder than his words. His silence -- rude and cowardly. If you can't take the heat, don't light the fire.

~~~~~~

When that happens … Run, baby, run!!!

Remember the song "What I did for Love" - Chorus Line
~~~~~~

10

Your Self-Love Must Always Be Stronger Than Your Desire To Be Loved By Others

Rhett

Let's talk about Rhett. Another online connection. We wrote back and forth, exchanged numbers, and talked often on the phone. It seemed we had many things in common. Eventually, we agreed to meet in person. Since he had an aging mother that he cared for, (How endearing, right?) I would travel to Wisconsin to meet him.

We deduced that I would take the high-speed ferry across Lake Michigan for the first meeting. That can be a bit risky (remember Wayne from Wisconsin, chapter 2?) since the weather is unpredictable over that large body of water. On one of my trips over, vomit bags were being given out as you boarded the boat! But on the day of this adventure, the lake is calm, and all seems fine.

After the two and a half-hour boat ride, I arrived at the Wisconsin dock, exited the boat, and didn't see Rhett anywhere! (Screech -- now what?) Within a few minutes (that felt like 20), I got a text saying he was running late (duh). He said he was only a few minutes out. Hmmm. Am I not as important to him as his words had indicated like Ryan? Was he with someone else the night before like Jacob? Is this how he operates? (*It's so hard to determine others 'behavior when you're triggered.*)

He finally pulled up, got out of his car, and gave me a big hug. That was nice. And imagine my surprise, he DOES look like his pictures! (That is risky, too, you know.) He played basketball in college and has kept his svelte physique. He looks good.

After we had a nice lunch, he wanted to show me around the area. We went to a couple of stores, and then stopped at a boutique where I tried on a dress. I exited the dressing room to show him. His eyes lit up!

"Yes!" He says.

He liked it. I took the dress to the counter for purchase. He stepped in and said he would buy it for me. How kind and much appreciated. He does mention that I paid for my own ferry ride to meet him. Maybe he felt a bit guilty about that. (Nah, probably not.)

We spent a few more hours in town. We enjoyed just perusing local establishments and then headed to a local pub. It was a place with a basketball hoop. We grabbed a drink, and Rhett immediately headed to the hoop and started shooting. He probably made four of the five shots he attempted. He did play basketball for University of Wisconsin after all, so he should be pretty good.

He tells me, "I want you to know what you have in me." What did that mean? I didn't catch on right away, but he was obviously very proud of himself. He pulled out his phone to show me college photos of himself on the court. (*I never thought to keep look-at-me-back-then photos handy.*)

Regardless of his ego, we had a lovely time. All too soon our time was over, and I sailed off into the sunrise, I'm headed east you know.

Since reciprocation is a quality I admire, it's his turn to visit me, right? That's when the excuses started rolling in. "Oh, my mother's caretaker is out sick. My business partner needs to meet with me. My cousin has an illness, my brother is living on the streets, and I have to find him."

Maybe all true, probably not. He was apparently taking care of a lot of people and things in his life. I wasn't high on that list.

I tried to be understanding, right? I was taught to forgive. In other words, ROLLOVER AND PLAY DEAD. It doesn't matter how someone else treats you, you forgive. What a load of crap. But that's what I did -- just went on pretending everything was fine for a long time.

I went back to visit him in Wisconsin three times before he graced me with his presence. I invited him to a black-tie event I needed to attend for my job. When I mentioned it to him, he seemed excited to join me. He told me how he owned his own tuxedo that still fit him perfectly. Apparently, he loved to show off his handsome self in a tuxedo. Fine by me. This event would be full of people who loved to do the same. He should fit right in.

Since Rhett had bailed on me many times with his many excuses, I was very worried on the day of the event. All day I was fretting. Will he show? Won't he show? But, alas, he was finally there: tall, dark, and handsome. He was a very gracious date. Be still, my heart. For the record, I looked pretty damn good myself in my silver Art Deco gown. He was kind enough to mention how beautiful I looked.

Back home and back to reality, the phone calls dwindled. He often had excuses for not calling. When I left a snide remark about this in a voicemail, he actually ghosted me for weeks (remember Josiah). So that's how this works. I see. I stand up for myself and get the silent treatment! Hmmmm.

So then he would promise to visit, then he couldn't make it, yes, no, maybe. Could I go his way? Well, maybe I can come your way. Well … blah, blah, blah. The yoyo effect has grabbed me in the past. Up, down, out, in, -- throw her a bone, don't talk to her. I've rationalized bad behavior many times in the past as I'm certain you've noticed.

Rhett was also an audiophile with a music room in his home. When I was remodeling my small lake house, I asked for his advice on purchasing speakers for my downstairs room. He was delighted to assist and promptly hopped on that task.

He said, "I have a pre-amp you can have since it all will eventually be ours anyway."

Yes, he had mentioned marriage a few times during our 2-½-year relationship. He then went on talking about speakers, amps, etc., most of which I did not know much about. He said all I needed to do was call so-and-so with my credit card; he would pick everything up, take the ferry to Michigan with the equipment, and get it all set up in my house for me. How nice, right?

I was at the dock waiting when he arrived. I see him walking toward me with a dolly full of large boxes. WTF. I greet him with a very quizzical look on my face, which he doesn't even notice.

Once we arrive at my house and get the boxes unloaded, I am rather upset. The speakers are approximately 3 feet high, and the amp and preamp are huge. This is not what I asked for or expected. Keep in mind this is a small, cottage-like house. He brought specific wires and connections, and he has very specific ways he wants things done.

All of my suggestions end up getting completely rebuffed or ignored. He is annoyed with any questions I raise since apparently, he's the expert. As he's getting things set up, he wants to rearrange the room so the speakers are two to three feet from the walls for the best sound. Well, that is a hell no.

I will spare you more details, but once everything is put together, he wants to run everything on my phone. He takes my phone and shows me a number of steps to follow. Since I'm a "do it" learner rather than a "hear it" learner, I tell him I'd like to try myself on my own phone with him watching over my shoulder. In a very exasperated tone, he tells me, "just watch me again."

Well, well, well…I do watch again, but I have shut down. None of this was what I wanted in the first place. He wasn't listening from the very beginning.

So, finally, I stopped listening, grabbed my phone back, and went upstairs. I was so done with his lies, excuses, ghosting, and never hearing what I wanted, needed, or said.

I went back downstairs after about 20 minutes, where he was still fussing with the equipment.

I said, "My mother has taken a fall. I need to get to her very soon because my sister needs help with her. I need you to leave as soon as possible."

Rhett said, "I understand, but can I get a bite to eat before I leave?"

What is with this guy? He belittles me, shames me, disrespects me, and now wants me to feed him?

The truth is, my mother did not fall, but I can't wait to get this guy out of my house and far away from my space. I felt like a child who had been naughty during this entire process, and it was all taking place in MY house.

He's got to go!

A few weeks later, I was contemplating a number of these experiences during a "cry my eyes out" pity party for myself. Luckily, just like Sleeping Beauty, I woke up. Unfortunately, it was not from a kiss by Prince Charming. I was lying on my sofa in a puddle of tears. I was thinking and saying negative things about Rhett, other previous people, and myself. I was a champion at negative self-talk. Damn! I then slapped myself a few times and reached for my dependable boyfriend: MacBook Air!

I bet you're thinking I wrote him a long nasty note, aren't you? I certainly have done that, as you have seen in the previous chapters. This time, however, I searched the internet for events I could and would do by myself.

Ah, yes. It could have been a luxurious vacation, like Paris, but I chose the Ashram in the Bahamas. In my hometown, that is a questionable alternative. Questions were, "Aren't you afraid to go by yourself? Does that mean you're not a Christian?" And I was blatantly told, "You'll go to Hell if you do that." Apparently, I'm a bit out of the norm. But off I went.

It was the best thing ever. The Ashram I chose was oceanfront on Paradise Island in the Bahamas. It was February, the weather was perfect, yoga was available twice daily, swimming in the ocean, healthy meals prepared for you, and I met a number of like-minded, wonderful people. These were people who did not question my judgment or self-care capabilities.

Since that time, I have been back to the Ashram twice. I have traveled to other locations to learn and experience challenges with limited fear. (I did get a bit lost taking the backroads to Breitenbush Hot Springs outside of Portland, OR, with no cell service. Scary).

I discovered that self-reflective workshops are a wonderful means of caring for oneself. At least for me. My self-reflection has helped me realize that I believed I needed a man to make me whole. I now realize I don't need a man to complete me. I want a man to love me as I am, and I will do the same for him. Compliment is the word I like to use. Compliment each other.

Our societal, local, or religious norms don't make us

whole. We make ourselves whole. It's hard to see our own flaws and beliefs, but in my humble opinion, it's very important. Being whole without a partner is very challenging in our society. But it can be done!

The Ashram in the Bahamas may not be the option you would choose, but I encourage you to find whatever works for you, with or without a partner by your side.

Amen

Namaste

Peace Out

Lovingly,

Scarlet